LE CORDON BLEU

HOME COLLECTION

·POTATOES·

MEREHURST

contents

recipe ratings ❀ easy ❀ ❀ a little more care needed ❀ ❀ ❀ more care needed

Potato salad with Parmesan and tomato

Potato salad is a perennial favourite—especially in summer—and can be enjoyed as a side dish, or simply on its own. This particular version is satisfying and flavoursome.

Preparation time 30 minutes
Total cooking time 35 minutes
Serves 4

6 medium to large salad potatoes, scrubbed
  (see Chef's tip)
I large tomato
I lettuce
I French shallot, finely chopped
chopped fresh chives, to serve
grated Parmesan, to serve

VINAIGRETTE
2 teaspoons mustard
I tablespoon white wine vinegar
100 ml (3 1/4 fl oz) olive oil
70 g (2 1/4 oz) Parmesan, grated

1 Place the potatoes in a large pan of salted water. Bring to the boil, then reduce the heat and simmer for 30–35 minutes, or until tender to the point of a knife. Remove and plunge into a bowl of iced water to stop them cooking. Peel the potatoes, then cut them into 1 cm (1/2 inch) cubes and set aside to cool.

2 Bring a small pan of water to the boil. With the point of a small sharp knife, score a small cross in the skin at the base of the tomato. Drop the tomato into the boiling water for 10 seconds, then plunge it into a bowl of cold water. Peel the skin away from the cross, then cut around and remove the stalk from the tomato. Slice the tomato into quarters, remove and discard the seeds and finely dice the flesh. Set aside.

3 To make the vinaigrette, mix the mustard and vinegar together in a small bowl and season to taste. Gradually pour in the oil in a thin steady stream, whisking until the mixture emulsifies and thickens. Stir in the grated Parmesan, then gently toss the potato cubes in the vinaigrette until well coated.

4 Arrange the lettuce leaves on six plates. Pile some potato salad in the centre and garnish each salad with a sprinkling of shallot, chives and diced tomato, then a little extra Parmesan and freshly ground black pepper.

Chef's tip Jersey royal, kipfler and pink fir apple are some potato varieties well suited for use in salads.

Potatoes à la boulangère

In the last century, kitchens were generally less well equipped than today, and most people, especially countryfolk, did not have ovens. In any case, working in the fields left little time to prepare a hot evening meal, so women would prepare a dish in the morning and leave it at the local bakery to cook and keep warm—hence the name for this meal, which translates in English as 'Baker's potatoes'.

Preparation time **20 minutes**
Total cooking time **1 hour**
Serves 4–5

4–5 medium potatoes
50 g (1³/4 oz) unsalted butter
1 onion, sliced
800 ml (26 fl oz) chicken stock or water
sprig of fresh thyme
1 bay leaf

1 Preheat the oven to moderately hot 200°C (400°F/ Gas 6). Peel and trim the potatoes, then thinly slice them using a sharp knife, or a mandolin set at 2 mm (1/8 inch) (see Chef's techniques, page 61). Place in a bowl of cold water until ready to use.

2 Place a large shallow pan or flameproof casserole dish over medium-low heat. Add the butter, then the onion and season well. Cover and cook, without browning, for about 5 minutes, or until soft and translucent. Drain the potato slices, then add them to the pan, stirring gently with a wooden spoon to coat them evenly with butter. Cook until hot—steam will begin to rise.

3 Add the stock, thyme and bay leaf. Stir once and bring to a simmer. Check the seasoning, then cover with lightly greased baking paper and bake for 45 minutes, or until the liquid is almost absorbed and the potatoes are soft. Pierce the baking paper with a roasting fork and lift carefully to avoid the hot steam. Serve the potatoes hot.

Chef's tip Adding a tablespoon of paprika and a little extra pepper when cooking the onions will give this dish a Hungarian flavour.

Byron potatoes

Memorable moments: potato patties dabbed with cream and coated with a layer of melted cheese!

Preparation time **15 minutes**
Total cooking time **1 hour 10 minutes**
Serves 4

4 large potatoes, scrubbed
100 g (3¹/4 oz) unsalted butter
2 tablespoons thick (double) cream
50 g (1³/4 oz) Cheddar, grated

1 Preheat the oven to moderately hot 200°C (400°F/ Gas 6). Prick the potatoes with a fork, place on a baking tray and bake for 45 minutes to 1 hour, or until cooked through and tender when tested with the point of a knife, or squeezed between finger and thumb.
2 While they are still hot, cut the potatoes in half. Using a metal spoon, scoop out the flesh. Mash lightly, stir in the butter, season to taste with salt and freshly ground black pepper, then allow to cool.
3 Sprinkle a little flour onto a work surface and, with floured hands, divide the mixture into four equal portions. Shape each portion into a ball, then gently press into round patties 2 cm (3/4 inch) thick. Transfer to an oiled baking tray. Preheat the grill to high.
4 Make an indentation 1 cm (¹/2 inch) deep in the centre of each patty with your thumb or the back of a teaspoon, then pour in some cream. Sprinkle the cheese over the patties, place under a hot grill and cook until the cheese is melted and browned.

Chef's tip Step 1 can be prepared in advance, or having shaped and made the indent, the patties can be left for a few hours until ready to finish.

Duchess potatoes

So simple, and so spectacular, these potato rosettes are regal fare indeed.

Preparation time **20 minutes**
Total cooking time **40 minutes**
Serves 4

4 medium potatoes, scrubbed
3 egg yolks
40 g (1¹/4 oz) unsalted butter
pinch of grated nutmeg

1 Preheat the oven to very hot 250°C (500°F/Gas 10). Place the potatoes in a large pan of salted water, bring to the boil, then reduce the heat and simmer for 30–35 minutes, or until tender to the point of a sharp knife. Drain and, while they are still hot, peel the potatoes, then purée them into a bowl (see Chef's techniques, page 62).
2 Using a wooden spoon, mix in the egg yolks and butter and season to taste with nutmeg and a pinch of salt. Mix until smooth.
3 Fit a pastry bag with a large star nozzle, fill it with the potato mixture, then pipe rosettes onto a buttered baking tray. Bake in the oven for 5 minutes, or until the rosettes are golden brown. Alternatively, brown them under a hot grill.

Chef's tip Duchess potatoes can be served in many delicious ways. For instance, decorative designs can be piped onto the edge of an ovenproof serving platter, or you could pipe out small 'nests' and fill them with a sauté of wild mushrooms or a creamy sauce. The rosettes can also be sprinkled with slivered almonds before baking.

Byron potatoes (top) and Duchess potatoes

Almond-dipped potato croquettes

The humble potato becomes a magical treat when rolled into croquettes and covered in a crisp and nutty coating. Made larger, they are perfect as a first course or lunch.

Preparation time **20 minutes**
Total cooking time **1 hour 20 minutes**
Serves **8**

4 large potatoes, scrubbed
45 g (1 1/2 oz) unsalted butter
2 egg yolks
pinch of grated nutmeg
oil, for deep-frying
100 g (3 1/4 oz) plain flour
2 eggs, lightly beaten
100 g (3 1/4 oz) ground almonds
100 g (3 1/4 oz) chopped almonds

1 Preheat the oven to moderately hot 190°C (375°F/Gas 5). Prick the potatoes several times with a fork to allow the steam to escape during baking, and so prevent bursting. Bake for 45 minutes to 1 hour, or until cooked through and tender to the point of a knife, or soft to the squeeze of forefinger and thumb.
2 Cut the potatoes in half and scoop the flesh into a small bowl. While the flesh is still warm, gently mash it, then stir in the butter, egg yolks, nutmeg, and salt and freshly ground black pepper to taste. Set aside to cool.
3 Preheat a deep-fat fryer or deep pan, one-third full of oil, to 180°C (350°F). Season the flour with salt and freshly ground black pepper, then spread out on a large plate. Place the lightly beaten whole eggs on a second plate. Mix together the ground and chopped almonds, and spread on a third plate.
4 With cupped hands, shape the potato mixture into small balls about 4 cm (1 1/2 inches) in diameter, then, between flat palms, roll the balls into cylinders about 6 cm (2 1/2 inches) long. Lay the croquettes in a row and, using a large palette knife, flatten both ends of the croquettes to make them of an equal length.
5 Coat the croquettes in the flour, beaten egg and then the almonds (see Chef's techniques, page 63), then deep-fry the croquettes in batches for 3–4 minutes (see Chef's techniques, page 63). Serve immediately.

Chef's tips Do not reheat or serve the croquettes covered, as their own steam will be trapped and they will become soggy.

Chopped almonds are also sold as nibbed almonds.

Home-made potato crisps

Home-made crisps traditionally accompany roasted meats and game, but they are just as good served with a light meal at lunch time.

Preparation time **15 minutes + 10 minutes soaking**
Total cooking time **10 minutes**
Serves 4

oil, for deep-frying
4 large floury potatoes, peeled

1 Preheat a deep-fat fryer or deep pan, one-third full of oil, to 180°C (350°F). Thinly slice the potatoes using a sharp knife, or a mandolin set at 2 mm (1/8 inch) (see Chef's techniques, page 61). Place the potato slices in cold water for 10 minutes to remove some of the sticky starch—this gives a crisper result.

2 Drain the slices and dry thoroughly on paper towels. Deep-fry in batches for about 3 minutes, or until golden (see Chef's techniques, page 63), stirring occasionally to keep the crisps separated and to help them colour evenly. Remove from the pan and drain on crumpled paper towels. Sprinkle the crisps with salt while they are still warm.

Chef's tip Paper towels that have been crumpled provide the best drainage for deep-fried foods, as the paper is more absorbent and has troughs for the oil to drain into. As the food is not resting on a flat, oily surface, the result is much crisper.

Rösti

Fried like a pancake and made from grated potato, rösti—a Swiss delicacy—can also be made using precooked potatoes for a quick and delicious dish.

Preparation time **15 minutes + cooling**
Total cooking time **45 minutes**
Serves 6

500 g (1 lb) large floury potatoes, scrubbed
25 ml (3/4 fl oz) oil
25 g (3/4 oz) unsalted butter
1 onion, thinly sliced

1 Preheat the oven to moderate 180°C (350°F/Gas 4). Place the potatoes in a large pan of salted water. Bring to the boil, reduce the heat and simmer for 10 minutes. Drain and leave the potatoes to cool completely. Peel the potatoes, then either grate them coarsely, or cut them into fine sticks.

2 In a non-stick, ovenproof frying pan, heat the oil and add the butter. Gently cook the onion until soft and transparent. Add the potato and season well. Stir for a few minutes, then press down gently with a wide spatula to make a thick, flat pancake. Increase the heat to high and brown the first side, then transfer the pan to the oven and bake for 15 minutes.

3 Loosen the pancake, turn it out onto a large plate, then return the pancake to the pan, browned-side-up. Take care not to break the pancake, and also be careful of your fingers as there may be some loose hot oil and butter. Return the pan to the oven and bake for another 10 minutes, then turn the pancake out onto a plate. Present whole, or cut into wedges like a cake.

Home-made potato crisps (top) and Rösti

Aurore potatoes

This ambrosial dish takes its name from the sauce. Aurore is the French word for dawn, and here it refers to a béchamel sauce with the addition of just enough tomato to tint it pink. Aurore potatoes are best enjoyed with simple, delicately flavoured dishes such as poached fish or chicken, or lightly smoked fish.

*Preparation time **20 minutes***
*Total cooking time **50 minutes***
Serves 4

500 g (1 lb) baby potatoes
sprig of fresh mint
250 g (8 oz) tomatoes
45 g (1¹/₂ oz) unsalted butter
1 clove garlic, crushed
1 teaspoon tomato paste
1 teaspoon paprika
3 tablespoons plain flour
300 ml (9¹/₂ fl oz) milk
2 tablespoons thick (double) cream

1 Scrape the thin skin from the potatoes and place them in a large pan of cold, salted water. Add the mint, bring to the boil, then reduce the heat and simmer for 10 minutes. Drain and set aside, discarding the mint.

2 Cut the tomatoes in half and scoop out the seeds with a teaspoon. Discard the seeds and roughly chop the tomato flesh; set aside.

3 Melt 15 g (¹/₂ oz) of the butter in a medium pan. Add the tomato flesh, garlic, tomato paste and paprika and cook over gentle heat for about 5 minutes, or until pulpy. Strain into a small bowl and set aside. Preheat the oven to moderate 180°C (350°F/Gas 4).

4 Melt the remaining butter in a heavy-based pan over medium-low heat. Sprinkle the flour over the base of the pan and cook for 1–2 minutes without browning, stirring all the while with a wooden spoon.

5 Slowly add the milk, whisking vigorously until the sauce begins to thicken. Whisk the sauce until it comes to the boil, then reduce the heat to low and cook gently for 3–4 minutes, or until the sauce coats the back of a spoon. If the sauce develops lumps, pass it through a fine sieve and then reheat it in a clean pan. Season to taste with salt and freshly ground black pepper, then stir in the tomato mixture and the cream. Adjust the seasoning if necessary.

6 Add the potatoes and shake the pan to coat them thoroughly in the sauce. Transfer the potatoes and sauce to a 1.5 litre ovenproof dish or casserole dish. Cover with aluminium foil and bake for 20 minutes, or until the potatoes are tender to the point of a knife.

Potato gaufrette baskets

Potato baskets are classic, impressive garnishes used to contain various treats such as soufflé potatoes, deep-fried herbs or diced vegetables.

Preparation time **10 minutes + 10 minutes soaking**
Total cooking time **20 minutes**
Makes 4 large baskets

2 large potatoes
oil, for deep-frying

1 Preheat a deep-fat fryer or deep pan, one-third full of oil, to 180°C (350°F). Peel the potatoes, then slice off the tops to help make the slices even.

2 Run the potatoes against a corrugated mandolin blade set at 1 mm. Discard the first slice, give the potato a quarter-turn to the left or right and cut the next slice. Repeat to cut more slices, giving a quarter-turn between each slice, and always turning in the same direction. Alternatively, thinly slice the potatoes using a sharp knife (see Chef's techniques, page 61). Place the slices in a bowl of cold water for 10 minutes to remove some of the starch—this gives a crisper finish. Drain and dry on paper towels or a tea towel.

3 Dip two round wire basket moulds—one about 7 cm (2³/4 inches) in diameter; the second a little smaller—into the hot oil for 5–10 seconds, then make the first potato basket following the method in the Chef's techniques on page 61. Deep-fry the potato basket for 3–5 minutes, or until crisp and golden brown (see Chef's techniques, page 63). Drain the potato basket, then unmould carefully and season with salt. Repeat with the remaining potato slices.

Chef's tip The moulds used in this recipe are also known as bird's nest moulds.

Potato croquettes

Croquette comes from a French word, croquer, meaning to crunch. The crisp exterior
of these croquettes harbours a splendid treat: a wonderful savoury surprise.

Preparation time **30** *minutes*
Total cooking time **45** *minutes*
Makes 14 croquettes

500 g (I lb) potatoes
pinch of grated nutmeg
20 g (³/4 oz) unsalted butter
I egg yolk
60 g (2 oz) plain flour
3 eggs, beaten
I tablespoon peanut (groundnut) oil
150 g (5 oz) dried breadcrumbs
oil, for deep-frying

SMOKED HAM CROQUETTES
100 g (3¹/4 oz) smoked ham, finely diced
50 g (I³/4 oz) grated Parmesan
50 g (I³/4 oz) cooked English spinach, chopped

OLIVE AND GOAT'S CHEESE CROQUETTES
60 g (2 oz) pitted black olives, chopped
150 g (5 oz) soft goat's cheese, cubed

1 Peel the potatoes and cut into even-sized pieces (either halve or quarter them, depending on their size). Place in a large pan of salted water. Bring to the boil, then reduce the heat and simmer for 30–35 minutes, or until tender to the point of a knife.

2 Drain the potatoes, shake them in the pan over low heat to dry, then purée them finely (see Chef's techniques, page 62). Season with salt, freshly ground black pepper and nutmeg, and stir in the butter and egg yolk. Spread the mixture out on a tray to cool.

3 To make the smoked ham croquettes, mix together the ham, Parmesan and spinach, season generously with

salt and freshly ground black pepper, then mix into half the potato mixture. Using floured hands, form the mixture into balls of about 2 tablespoons each, then roll on a floured surface into cylinders 6 cm (2¹/2 inches) long. Cover and refrigerate until ready to use.

4 To make the olive and goat's cheese croquettes, mix the olives and goat's cheese together and set aside. Make the croquettes as above using the remaining potato mixture, then using your fingers, press each croquette out into a rectangle. Press your index finger along the centre lengthways to form a ridge, then line the olive and goat's cheese mixture along the centre, but not all the way to the ends. Fold the ends over, then draw up the sides to fully enclose the filling, and roll to form a cylinder. Cover and refrigerate the croquettes until ready to use.

5 Preheat a deep-fat fryer or deep pan, one-third full of oil, to 180°C (350°F). Season the flour with salt and freshly ground black pepper, then spread out on a tray. In a bowl, mix together the beaten eggs and the peanut oil. Spread the dried breadcrumbs on a large sheet of greaseproof paper.

6 Coat the croquettes in the flour, egg and breadcrumbs (see Chef's techniques, page 63). Deep-fry in batches for 3–4 minutes, or until an even golden brown (see Chef's techniques, page 63). Serve immediately.

Chef's tips Make sure the potatoes are well dried in step 2, as moisture build-up will cause the croquettes to split and absorb more oil.

Always shake off (or press on) excess breadcrumbs, or they will fall into the oil during frying: they will then burn and cling to the croquettes as unsightly specks.

Also, spreading the breadcrumbs on a large piece of paper helps you coat the croquettes without getting crumbed and messy fingers.

Gratin dauphinois

This famous dish—a creamy gratin cooked in milk—derives from the mountainous region of Dauphiné near the French–Italian border.

Preparation time **30 minutes**
Total cooking time **1 hour**
Serves 4 as a side dish

500 g (1 lb) potatoes
500 ml (16 fl oz) milk
pinch of grated nutmeg
100 ml (3¼ fl oz) thick (double) cream
1 clove garlic, crushed or finely chopped
100 g (3¼ oz) Swiss cheese, grated

1 Preheat the oven to warm 170°C (325°F/Gas 3). Peel and trim the potatoes, then slice them thinly using a sharp knife, or mandolin set at 2 mm (⅛ inch) (see Chef's techniques, page 61). Place in a pan, cover with milk, then season with salt, pepper and nutmeg.
2 Place over medium-low heat and simmer gently for about 5 minutes, or until the potato is almost cooked, yet still firm. Strain and set the milk aside. Rub a 20 x 16 cm (8 x 6½ inch) ovenproof dish with butter, then evenly arrange the potato slices in the dish.
4 Reheat the milk and allow it to simmer for a few minutes. Stir in the cream and garlic, bring back to a simmer and check the seasoning. Simmer for a few more minutes, then pour the milk over the potato. Sprinkle with the grated cheese and bake in the oven for 35–45 minutes, or until the potato is tender and the top is nicely browned.

Chef's tip Be sure to season the sauce quite generously or the dish may taste a little bland.

Potato gnocchi

These popular little dumplings may be served as an entrée, as a main course with salad, or even to accompany roast meat.

Preparation time **30 minutes**
Total cooking time **50 minutes**
Serves 4–6

1 kg (2 lb) floury potatoes, scrubbed
220 g (7 oz) plain flour
1 teaspoon salt
small pinch of ground nutmeg

1 Place the potatoes in a large pan of salted water. Bring to the boil, then reduce the heat and simmer for 30–35 minutes, or until the potatoes are tender to the point of a sharp knife. Drain and leave to cool a little before removing the skins.
2 Purée the potatoes directly onto a lightly floured surface (see Chef's techniques, page 62). Sift the flour, salt and nutmeg onto the warm potato mash and work together—take care not to overwork the mixture or the texture will become gluey. Clean the surface and lightly flour again. Taking a little dough at a time, roll the mixture out into 2 cm (3/4 inch) lengths.
3 Bring a large pan of salted water to the boil and gently lower in the gnocchi. Do not overcrowd the pan or the gnocchi will stick together—you may have to cook them in several batches. When the gnocchi float to the surface, lift them out with a slotted spoon and place in a lightly oiled serving dish. Serve with a hot tomato pasta sauce and grated cheese.

Chef's tip King Edward and sebago potatoes are ideal for use in this dish.

Gratin dauphinois (top) with Potato gnocchi

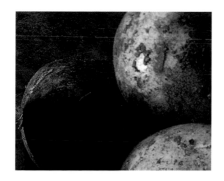

Roast potatoes

Meals involving roasted meats are never quite the same without crisp, golden roast potatoes. Even the simplest ingredients—olive oil, rosemary or salt—will further enhance their wonderful flavour.

Preparation time **15 minutes**
Total cooking time **50 minutes**
Serves **4**

1 kg (2 lb) floury potatoes
oil, for cooking

1 Preheat the oven to moderately hot 190°C (375°F/ Gas 5). Peel the potatoes and cut them into evenly sized pieces—halve or quarter them depending on their size. Place in a large pan of salted water, bring to the boil, then reduce the heat and simmer for about 5 minutes. Drain, then while the potatoes are still hot, hold each one in a cloth and lightly scratch the surface with a fork. Return to the pan and cover to keep hot.

2 Preheat a roasting pan over high heat and add oil to a depth of about 1 cm (1/2 inch). As the oil just starts to smoke, add the potatoes in a single layer. Roll them in the hot oil to seal all sides. Bake for 40 minutes, or until the potatoes are golden, turning and basting frequently with the oil. Drain on crumpled paper towels, sprinkle with salt and serve while still hot.

Chef's tips King Edward, spunta and sebago potatoes are perfect for roasting.

Boiling potatoes prior to roasting removes excess sticky starch from the surface, leaving them dry and crisp; scratching the surface contributes texture to that crispness. Rolling hot potatoes in hot oil will then seal them nicely, leaving the centres floury and oil free.

If the potatoes are to accompany a roasted meat, instead of cooking them in a separate pan, place them in the hot fat around the meat as it cooks. This will give a most delicious flavour.

For special occasions, shave off the square edges. The rounded potatoes will roll easily in the pan for all-over colour and crispness: the secret of the perfect roast potato.

Dauphine potatoes

Puffed and golden, dauphine potatoes—balls of puréed potato mixed with choux pastry—are a spectacular accompaniment to grilled or roast meat or game, and are especially lovely with poultry.

Preparation time **30 minutes**
Total cooking time **1 hour**
Makes 10

1 kg (2 lb) floury potatoes
oil, for deep-frying

CHOUX PASTRY
50 g (1³/4 oz) unsalted butter
70 g (2¹/4 oz) plain flour
2 eggs, lightly beaten

1 Peel the potatoes and cut into evenly sized pieces. Place in a large pan of salted water. Bring to the boil, then reduce the heat and simmer for 30–35 minutes, or until tender to the point of a knife. Drain.

2 Shake the potatoes in the pan over low heat to dry off any excess moisture, then purée them (see Chef's techniques, page 62). Transfer to a bowl, cover to keep warm and set aside. Preheat a deep-fat fryer or deep pan, one-third full of oil, to 170°C (325°F).

3 To make the choux pastry, place the butter with a pinch of salt and 125 ml (4 fl oz) water in a deep pan. Bring to the boil, then remove from the heat and immediately add all the flour, stirring to combine with a wooden spoon. Return the pan to low heat and cook, stirring constantly, until the mixture rolls off the sides of the pan. Remove from the heat to cool slightly, so the eggs will not cook when they are added.

4 Gradually add the eggs a little at a time, beating well between each addition. (The mixture will loosen with each addition, but thicken with beating.) You may not need to add the whole quantity of eggs: stop when the mixture drops freely from the spoon with a slight flick of the wrist.

5 Mix in the potato purée until just combined and season with salt to taste. Allow to cool, then roll into small balls about 3 cm (1¹/4 inches) in diameter. Deep-fry the potato balls in batches until golden brown (see Chef's techniques, page 63). Serve immediately.

Chef's tip Wholemeal flour can be used instead of plain flour in savoury choux pastry recipes.

Potato fans with bacon and Parmesan

Bursting with flavour, these easy potato fans are superb with fish, game or chicken.

Preparation time **20 minutes**
Total cooking time **1 hour 15 minutes**
Serves 6

6 medium potatoes
2 rashers bacon, chopped
1 garlic clove, crushed
1 litre chicken stock
40 g (1 1/4 oz) Parmesan, grated

1 Preheat the oven to warm 170°C (325°F/Gas 3). Peel the potatoes and cut into hasselbacks, following the method in the Chef's techniques on page 61. Place a small piece of bacon between each potato slice.
2 Butter a roasting pan and add the crushed garlic. Season the potatoes with salt and freshly ground black pepper, and place them flat-side-down in the pan. Pour in the stock to come no more than about halfway up the potatoes.
3 Heat the pan on the stove top and bring the stock to a gentle simmer, then transfer to the oven and bake for 20 minutes. Sprinkle the cheese over the potatoes and bake for 30–40 minutes, or until the potatoes are golden and just soft to the point of a sharp knife.

Chef's tip The potato trimmings may be used to make soup or mashed potatoes.

Caviar-filled potatoes

These elegantly dressed potatoes are so simple to prepare, but will add a touch of luxury to any special dinner party affair.

Preparation time **10 minutes**
Total cooking time **25 minutes**
Serves 4

8 small round potatoes
500 ml (16 fl oz) fish stock
120 g (4 oz) caviar
80 g (2 3/4 oz) crème fraîche or sour cream

1 Peel the potatoes, then neatly slice off one end to enable the potatoes to stand upright. Hollow out the centres using an apple corer, starting from the top but not reaching through to the base. (This cavity will hold the filling.) Neaten the rough edges using a small, sharp knife.
2 Butter the base of a pan. Add the potatoes and cover with the fish stock. Bring to the boil, then reduce the heat and simmer for 20–25 minutes, or until tender to the point of a sharp knife or skewer.
3 Drain the potatoes well, then fill the holes in the centre with a mound of caviar. Top with a teaspoon of crème fraîche or sour cream and a little caviar.

Chef's tip If caviar is not readily available, lumpfish roe is a perfectly suitable and less expensive alternative. Keta or salmon roe will provide a wonderful variation in colour and flavour.

Potato fans with bacon and Parmesan (top) with
Caviar-filled potatoes

Delmonico potatoes

This recipe was created and named after the chef and owner of a nineteenth-century restaurant of the same name.

Preparation time **30 minutes**
Total cooking time **30 minutes**
Serves 4

4 medium potatoes
350 ml (11 fl oz) milk
50 g (1³/4 oz) fresh breadcrumbs

1 Preheat the oven to moderate 180°C (350°F/Gas 4). Peel the potatoes, cut them into cubes and place in a pan with the milk. Season with salt and freshly ground black pepper.

2 Bring the mixture to the boil, then remove from the heat. Transfer to a 1.5 litre ovenproof oval baking dish measuring 20 x 16 cm (8 x 6¹/2 inches), spreading out the potatoes in an even layer. The milk should almost cover the potatoes—spoon some milk off, or add a little more if needed.

3 Evenly sprinkle the breadcrumbs over the top of the potatoes, all the way to the edge. Stand for 5 minutes for the breadcrumbs to absorb the milk.

4 Transfer to the oven and bake for 20 minutes, or until the top is an even golden brown. Leave to stand for 10–15 minutes before serving.

Chef's tips For added flavour, mix 2 tablespoons of grated cheese with the breadcrumbs before sprinkling them over the potatoes.

For a delightful and colourful variation, replace the potatoes with the same quantity of sweet potatoes. Due to their higher water content, the sweet potatoes should be baked in a deeper dish. Also allow for a slightly longer cooking time.

Fondant potatoes

*The golden colour of these potatoes and
their absorption of stock during cooking makes
them a flavoursome side dish to complement
any chicken dish or roasted meat.*

Preparation time **30 minutes**
Total cooking time **40 minutes**
Serves 2

4 medium potatoes
500 ml (16 fl oz) chicken stock
50 g (1³/4 oz) unsalted butter, melted

1 Preheat the oven to moderate 180°C (350°F/ Gas 4).
Peel the potatoes, then using a small knife or potato
peeler, turn each potato into a uniform shape, following
the method in the Chef's techniques on page 62.

2 Place the potatoes in a shallow ovenproof dish. Pour
in the chicken stock to come halfway up the sides of
the potatoes—the actual quantity of stock required will
vary according to the size of the dish the potatoes are
cooked in.

3 Brush the tops of the potatoes with a little melted
butter, sprinkle them lightly with salt, then bake in the
oven for 30–40 minutes, or until golden brown and
tender to the point of a sharp knife. Carefully lift the
potatoes out of the stock and serve while hot.

Chef's tip You can cook this dish without turning the
potatoes, providing the potatoes are of an even size. The
potatoes are turned simply for presentation.

Maxim's potatoes

*Maxim's is a famous Parisian restaurant. The fancy
presentation of this dish recalls its elegance.*

Preparation time **15 minutes**
Total cooking time **15 minutes**
Serves 4

600 g (1¹/4 lb) small potatoes
125 g (4 oz) clarified butter (see page 60)

1 Preheat the oven to very hot 240°C (475°F/Gas 9).
Peel and trim the potatoes and thinly slice using a sharp
knife, or a mandolin set at 2 mm (¹/8 inch) (see Chef's
techniques, page 61). Toss with salt.

2 Heat the clarified butter; pour half onto a baking tray.
Place a potato slice on the baking tray (this will be the
centre of the round) and arrange five or six overlapping
slices over the top. Repeat with the remaining slices and
brush with the remaining butter. Bake for 6–8 minutes,
or until the edges are brown. Turn. Cook for 2–3 minutes,
or until golden on both sides, with very crispy edges.
Cool on a wire rack for 5 minutes, then pat dry.

3 Alternatively, arrange the slices in a cold non-stick
frying pan. Generously drizzle the butter over and
around the circles and place over medium heat. Gently
shake the pan as it heats to prevent sticking. As they
cook, the circles will lift up and float in the butter.
Once the edges are coloured, turn the potatoes and
cook for 1–2 minutes, then drain on a rack.

4 To reheat, place on a wire rack in a hot oven for
2–3 minutes. Serve immediately.

Hasselback potatoes

This is an attractive and hearty way to serve potatoes. The deep cuts in the potatoes cook into crisp layers, beneath an appetising topping of browned breadcrumbs and cheese. Serve hot with roasted beef, lamb, game or poultry.

Preparation time **10 minutes**
Total cooking time **45 minutes**
Serves 6

6 evenly sized potatoes
30 g (1 oz) unsalted butter
1 tablespoon dried breadcrumbs
2 tablespoons grated strong cheese (such as mature Cheddar or Parmesan)

1 Preheat the oven to hot 220°C (425°F/Gas 7). Oil a roasting tin or ovenproof dish and set aside.

2 Peel the potatoes to approximately the same size, then slice them into hasselbacks, following the method in the Chef's techniques on page 61. Place the potatoes, sliced-side-up, in the dish. Sprinkle with salt and pepper, dot with the butter, then roast for 30 minutes.

4 Remove from the oven and baste with the melted butter. Sprinkle with the breadcrumbs and cheese, then roast for a further 15 minutes, or until the potatoes are tender to the point of a sharp knife.

Chef's tip To enhance the flavour when serving with roasted meats, sprinkle some chopped fresh rosemary or thyme into the cheese and breadcrumb topping.

Bourbonnais pie

The inhabitants of the French province of Bourbonnais are renowned as hearty eaters, especially fond of vegetable dishes and thick vegetable soups. This pie is a superb ambassador for the region's cuisine.

Preparation time 35 minutes + 30 minutes chilling
Total cooking time 1 hour 30 minutes
Serves 4

SHORTCRUST PASTRY
200 g (6¹/2 oz) plain flour
1¹/2 teaspoons salt
100 g (3¹/4 oz) unsalted butter, chopped
1 egg, lightly beaten

200 g (6¹/2 oz) potatoes, scrubbed
120 g (4 oz) bacon, cut into small cubes
100 ml (3¹/4 fl oz) thick (double) cream
3 egg yolks
90 g (3 oz) grated Swiss cheese or Cheddar

1 To make the shortcrust pastry, sift the flour and salt into a bowl. Using your fingertips, rub in the butter until the flour is evenly coloured and sandy in texture. Make a well in the centre, then add the beaten egg and a tablespoon of water. Mix well, shape the dough into a ball, wrap in plastic wrap and rest in the refrigerator for 30 minutes.

2 Preheat the oven to moderately hot 200°C (400°F/ Gas 6). Place the potatoes in a large pan of salted water and bring to the boil. Reduce the heat and simmer for 30–35 minutes, or until the potatoes are tender to the point of a knife. Drain and cool, then peel, slice thinly and set aside in a bowl.

3 Place the bacon in a small pan and cover with cold water. Bring to the boil, then drain, refresh in cold water and pat dry. Heat a little oil in a pan and gently brown the bacon. Drain on paper towels and add to the potato.

4 Place the cream in a pan and simmer until reduced by half. Set aside to cool. Whisk in two of the egg yolks and pour over the bacon and potato. Add the cheese and mix gently until combined. Season to taste.

5 Halve the dough and roll each portion into a 20 cm (8 inch) round, 2 mm (1/8 inch) thick. Place one round of pastry on a buttered baking tray. Spread the potato mixture over the top, leaving a 2.5 cm (1 inch) border. Whisk the remaining egg yolk with 2 teaspoons water and lightly brush the mixture over the border: it should be moist, but not wet.

6 Completely cover the filling with the second round of pastry. (Avoid stretching the pastry, as this can cause shrinking and leakage during baking.) Seal the edges, then fold the outer edge inwards, working around the pie to resemble a braid. Brush with more egg glaze.

7 Pierce the centre of the pie with the tip of a knife and enlarge the hole until it is 1 cm (1/2 inch) wide. Brush with a second coat of egg glaze, transfer to the oven and bake for 20–30 minutes, or until golden.

Sautéed potatoes

This is such a simple way to prepare potatoes, yet it remains a firm family favourite.

Preparation time **20 minutes**
Total cooking time **20 minutes**
Serves 4

3 medium floury potatoes
3 tablespoons oil, for frying
40 g (1 1/4 oz) unsalted butter

1 Peel the potatoes and cut into 1.5 cm (5/8 inch) cubes. Place in a bowl of cold water until ready to use.
2 Drain the potato cubes and pat them dry—this will remove any excess starch that may make the potatoes stick to the frying pan.
3 Heat a large non-stick frying pan over medium-high heat. Add the oil. When the oil is hot, add the dried potato cubes and stir or toss to evenly coat them with the oil. Tossing regularly, cook for 10–15 minutes, or until the potatoes are well coloured all over and cooked through. Pour them into a sieve to drain off the oil.
4 Melt the butter in the same frying pan, then add the potato cubes once again. Toss them in the pan until evenly coated with the butter, then season to taste with salt and freshly ground black pepper.

Mashed potatoes

There are as many versions of mashed potato as there are cooks. This mash is wonderfully creamy.

Preparation time **10 minutes**
Total cooking time **35 minutes**
Serves 4

4 medium floury potatoes
250 ml (8 fl oz) milk or cream
20 g (3/4 oz) unsalted butter or margarine

1 Peel the potatoes, cut into quarters and place in a large pan of salted water. Bring to the boil, then reduce the heat and simmer for 30–35 minutes, or until tender to the point of a knife.
2 Heat the milk or cream to boiling point, then remove from the heat and set aside.
3 Drain the potatoes and transfer to a large heat-resistant bowl. Mash with a large fork or potato masher, gradually mixing in enough butter and hot milk to give a good consistency, ensuring there are no lumps. Season to taste with salt and freshly ground black pepper.

Chef's tip To vary the flavour, steep your favourite herbs in the hot milk or cream, or purée and mix in other root vegetables. Olive oil can replace the butter.

Sautéed potatoes (top) and Mashed potatoes

Potato flans

*While the term 'flan' is generally taken to mean an open pastry tart, in France and Spain
it also describes a custard that is made in a mould, turned out and served cold. These flans,
flavoured with herbs and set with eggs, transform potatoes into a delicate side dish.*

Preparation time **30 minutes**
Total cooking time **1 hour**
Serves 4

8 small potatoes, about 100 g (3 1/4 oz) each
2 tablespoons sour cream or thick (double) cream
60 g (2 oz) unsalted butter, melted
2 eggs
pinch of grated nutmeg
1 tablespoon chopped fresh parsley or chives

1 Preheat the oven to moderately hot 200°C (400°F/ Gas 6). Rinse the potatoes in cold water, then wrap in foil without drying them. Bake for 30–40 minutes, or until tender to the point of a knife. While still hot, peel the potatoes and purée them into a bowl (see Chef's techniques, page 62): there should be about 400 g (12 3/4 oz) of purée. Place the bowl in a shallow pan of hot water to keep the purée warm.

2 Lightly brush four 125 ml (4 fl oz) ramekin moulds with butter, then refrigerate. Line a baking dish with two layers of paper towels and set aside.

3 Place the cream in a pan, bring to the boil, then remove from the heat.

4 Using a wooden spoon, mix the melted butter into the potato purée, scraping down the sides of the bowl. Mix in the eggs one at a time, season to taste with nutmeg, salt and freshly ground black pepper, then scrape down the sides again. Mix well, stirring in the parsley or chives. Add the cream last, mixing only just enough to blend it in, as overmixing will cause the cream to separate into butter.

5 Divide the mixture among the chilled moulds, filling them completely, and place in the prepared baking dish. Cover each mould with a round of buttered baking paper, half-fill the baking dish with boiling water and transfer to the oven. Bake for 20 minutes, or until a knife inserted into the centre of the moulds comes out clean. Carefully remove the moulds from the baking dish and allow to stand for 10–15 minutes before unmoulding.

Chef's tip Sweet potatoes can be used in this recipe instead of regular potatoes. Bake them in the oven for about 1 hour, or until tender, then follow the directions for regular potatoes.

Potato and corn chowder

While this hearty soup is not a true chowder as it contains no clams or fish, the word 'chowder' well describes its texture, which is thick and rich.

Preparation time **25 minutes**
Total cooking time **45 minutes**
Serves **4**

I tablespoon oil
100 g (3¹/4 oz) bacon, chopped into 5 mm
 (¹/4 inch) cubes
300 g (10 oz) potatoes, peeled and cut into 5 mm
 (¹/2 inch) cubes
400 g (12³/4 oz) corn kernels, fresh, frozen or canned
I litre chicken stock or water
500 ml (16 fl oz) thick (double) cream
I tablespoon chopped fresh coriander leaves

1 Heat the oil in a large pot, then brown the bacon cubes over low heat for 6–9 minutes. Add the potato and corn and cook for 3–5 minutes, or until the corn and potato juices have evaporated.
2 Add the chicken stock or water, bring to the boil, then reduce the heat and simmer for 25 minutes, or until the potatoes are tender to the point of a sharp knife. Add the cream and simmer for another 5 minutes, then season to taste. Stir in the coriander just before serving.

Chef's tip A diced red capsicum (pepper) can be added with the potatoes and corn for added colour, and a finely chopped clove of garlic with the stock for extra flavour.

Potage Parmentier

Antoine Augustin Parmentier was an eighteenth-century food writer and economist, said to have converted the French to potatoes. Before this time, potatoes were widely held to be devil's food!

Preparation time **15 minutes**
Total cooking time **45 minutes**
Serves **4**

2 medium potatoes
2 small leeks, white part only
60 g (2 oz) unsalted butter

1 Peel the potatoes, cut them into quarters lengthways and then slice thinly. Keep in cold water until ready to use. Trim the roots off the leeks, then cut each leek in half lengthways and slice thinly.
2 In a large pot, melt the butter, add the leeks and cook over low heat for about 8 minutes, or until the leeks are soft and all the liquid has evaporated. Add the sliced potatoes and 1.25 litres water. Bring to the boil, reduce the heat, and simmer for 30 minutes, or until the potatoes are tender to the point of a sharp knife, skimming off any fat or foam that floats to the surface. Season to taste with salt and freshly ground black pepper.

Chef's tip This soup may be served just the way it is, but if you prefer a creamier texture, purée the soup in a blender or food processor, then strain and bring gently to the boil before serving.

Potato and corn chowder (bottom) with Potage Parmentier

Spiced Indian potatoes

These mildly spicy potatoes are an exotic alternative to everyday side dishes. Try serving them cold with grilled meats in place of potato salad.

Preparation time **30 minutes**
Total cooking time **40 minutes**
Serves 4

500 g (1 lb) baby potatoes
2 tablespoons olive oil
1 onion, chopped
1 teaspoon grated fresh ginger
1/2 teaspoon ground turmeric
1 green chilli, seeded and chopped
1 teaspoon ground cumin
1 tablespoon chopped fresh coriander leaves

1 Preheat the oven to moderate 180°C (350°F/Gas 4). Scrape the thin skin from the potatoes and place them in a large pan of salted water. Bring to the boil, reduce the heat and simmer for 10 minutes. Drain the potatoes and set aside.

2 Heat the oil in a large frying pan over medium heat, then cook the onion for 2 minutes, or until translucent. Add the ginger, turmeric, chilli, cumin and a pinch of salt and cook for 1 minute more, stirring constantly.

3 Add the potatoes and toss them in the spices until well coated. Transfer to an ovenproof dish, shaking any remaining spice mixture over the top. Bake for about 20 minutes, or until tender to the point of a sharp knife. Sprinkle with coriander just before serving. Serve hot or cold with grilled meats and Indian dishes.

Potato pancakes

Similar to blinis, these pancakes are delicious served with smoked salmon, caviar, sour cream and chives. For a surprising variation in flavour, add some chopped fresh herbs or bacon with the cream.

*Preparation time **15 minutes + 45 minutes cooling***
*Total cooking time **1 hour 30 minutes***
*Makes **12 large pancakes***

4 medium floury potatoes
315 ml (10 fl oz) milk
3 tablespoons plain flour
3 eggs
3 tablespoons sour cream or thick (double) cream
pinch of nutmeg
1 egg white
oil or clarified butter (see page 60), for cooking

1 Preheat the oven to slow 150°C (300°F/Gas 2). Peel the potatoes and cut into quarters. Place in a large pan of salted water. Bring to the boil, then reduce the heat and simmer for 35 minutes, or until tender to the point of a knife. Drain and rinse in cold water, then dry them in the oven for 15 minutes. Purée the potatoes until completely smooth (see Chef's techniques, page 62), and keep warm in the oven.

2 Place 10 ice cubes in a large bowl. Add 500 ml (16 fl oz) water, place a smaller bowl inside and set aside.

3 Bring the milk to the boil. Add the potato and stir with a wooden spoon until the mixture is liquid enough to slide off the spoon. Pour into the bowl in the ice bath, and stir until the mixture stops steaming. Leave for at least 45 minutes, or until completely cooled.

4 Sift the flour over the mixture and gently stir in. Mix in the eggs one at a time, ensuring each egg is completely mixed in before adding the next. Stir in the cream, then salt, pepper and nutmeg to taste. Beat the egg white in a small dry bowl until stiff peaks form, then gently fold into the potato and egg: the mixture should be the same consistency as a pancake batter. If it seems too runny, add another beaten egg white.

5 Preheat a blini pan or small crêpe pan over medium-low heat. Wipe the hot pan with 2 tablespoons of oil or clarified butter, and quickly pour in 80 ml (2³/4 fl oz) of batter. Cook until the surface is bubbly, and the edges have set and won't move when the pan is jiggled, then turn and cook the other side. Drain on paper towels and keep warm while cooking the other pancakes.

Lyonnaise potatoes

Lyon is famous for its gourmet cuisine. Glazed onions and chopped parsley are the distinctive Lyonnais features of this simple sautéed dish.

Preparation time **30 minutes**
Total cooking time **30 minutes**
Serves 4–6

4 medium potatoes
80 g (2³/4 oz) unsalted butter
I small onion, finely chopped
I tablespoon finely chopped fresh parsley

1 Peel and trim the potatoes, following the method in the Chef's techniques for slicing by hand on page 61. Discard the trimmings. Thinly slice the potatoes using a sharp knife, or a mandolin set at 2 mm (¹/8 inch) (see Chef's techniques, page 61). Place the slices in a bowl and cover with cold water until ready to use.

2 Heat a heavy-based pan over medium heat. Add half the butter and all the onion and season well. Cook, without browning, until the onions have become soft and translucent. Remove from the pan and set aside.

3 Drain the potato slices well and pat dry. Add the remaining butter to the pan. When it has completely melted, sprinkle the potato slices over the base of the pan, then toss or mix until evenly coated. Cook over medium heat, tossing regularly, until the edges are golden brown and the slices are cooked through. Return the onion to the pan, add the chopped parsley and toss well. Check the seasoning before serving.

Potato griddle scones

These scones are delicious served with grilled bacon—or simply butter, jam or honey—as a leisurely brunch or breakfast.

Preparation time **10 minutes**
Total cooking time **45 minutes**
Makes 12 scones

500 g (I lb) potatoes
60 g (2 oz) unsalted butter, at room temperature
60 g (2 oz) plain flour
I teaspoon baking powder
large pinch of grated nutmeg

1 Peel the potatoes and place them in a large pan of salted water. Bring to the boil, then reduce the heat and simmer for 30–35 minutes. Drain well, then return to the pan to dry over low heat

2 Purée the potatoes into a smooth mash (see Chef's techniques, page 62), then beat in the butter. Sift the flour, baking powder, nutmeg and some salt into a bowl. Add the potato purée and, using a round-bladed knife, bring the mixture together. You will need to use the mixture at once as baking powder is activated by moisture and warmth.

3 Pat out the mixture to a 1.5 cm (⁵/8 inch) thickness. Using a 4 cm (1¹/2 inch) plain cutter, cut out 12 rounds. Heat a heavy-based frying pan or griddle over medium heat and dust lightly with flour. Cook the scones for about 8 minutes, or until cooked through, turning after 4 minutes. Serve warm.

Lyonnaise potatoes (top) with Potato griddle scones

Potato and Jerusalem artichoke casserole

The Jerusalem artichoke is not a true artichoke, but a variety of sunflower. It resembles a ginger root and has a nutty sweet taste, which greatly enhances the flavour of this dish. This is an ideal casserole to serve with lamb or veal.

Preparation time **35 minutes**
Total cooking time **55 minutes**
Serves 4–6

250 g (8 oz) baby potatoes
500 g (I lb) Jerusalem artichokes, peeled and trimmed to an even size (see Chef's tip)
500 ml (16 fl oz) milk
45 g (1¹/₂ oz) unsalted butter
250 g (8 oz) button mushrooms, stalks removed
30 g (1 oz) plain flour
2 tablespoons thick (double) cream
pinch of grated nutmeg

1 Scrape the thin peel from the potatoes. Place the potatoes in a large pan of salted water, bring to the boil, then reduce the heat and simmer for 10 minutes. Drain and set aside. Place the Jerusalem artichokes in a pan, pour in the milk, bring to the boil, then reduce the heat and gently simmer for 10 minutes, or until just tender. Drain the artichokes and reserve the liquid.

2 Melt a third of the butter in a heavy-based pan over high heat. Add the mushrooms, cook for 1 minute, then remove from the pan and set aside. Wipe the pan clean with paper towels and heat the remaining butter over medium-low heat. Sprinkle the flour over the base of the pan and cook for 1–2 minutes without colouring, stirring constantly with a wooden spoon.

3 Slowly add the reserved milk, whisking vigorously to prevent lumps forming. Over medium heat, whisk the mixture until it comes to the boil, then reduce the heat to low and gently cook the sauce for about 4 minutes, or until it coats the back of the spoon. If the sauce develops lumps, pass it through a fine sieve into a clean pan and reheat. Add the cream and season to taste with salt, freshly ground black pepper and nutmeg. Preheat the oven to moderate 180°C (350°F/Gas 4).

4 Transfer the potatoes, artichokes and mushrooms to a flameproof casserole dish and cover with the sauce. Shake gently to ensure the vegetables are well coated. Bring to the boil, then remove from the heat. Cover, then transfer to the oven and bake for 15–20 minutes.

Chef's tip As you peel the artichokes, place them in a bowl of cold water with a few drops of lemon juice or vinegar to prevent discolouring. Rinse the artichokes before using.

Jacket potatoes

Jacket potatoes are always a welcome side dish, yet they can also be transformed into a magnificent main course with the addition of an infinite range of fillings. Here are just a few.

Preparation time **20 minutes**
Total cooking time **1 hour 15 minutes**
Serves 4

4 medium floury potatoes
oil, for deep-frying

SOUR CREAM AND CHIVE FILLING
500 ml (16 fl oz) sour cream
2 tablespoons chopped fresh chives

CHEESE AND BACON FILLING
250 g (8 oz) Cheddar or Swiss cheese, grated
3 rashers cooked bacon, coarsely chopped

GREEK-STYLE FILLING
90 g (3 oz) pitted black olives, sliced or chopped
250 g (8 oz) feta cheese, diced

ROASTED GARLIC AND SOUR CREAM FILLING
16 cloves garlic, roasted and peeled (see Chef's tips)
500 ml (16 fl oz) sour cream

1 Preheat the oven to moderate 180°C (350°F/Gas 4). Trim any spots or eyes from the potatoes, leaving the skin as intact as possible. Rub the potatoes with oil and pierce with a fork. Bake for 1 hour, or until easily pierced to the centre with the point of a small, sharp knife.

2 Cut the potatoes in half lengthways. Scoop out most of the flesh with a small spoon, leaving a shell about 5 mm (1/4 inch) thick. Set the potatoes aside.

3 Preheat a deep-fat fryer or deep pan, one-third full of oil, to 180°C (350°F). Lightly mash the potato flesh with a fork, then mix through your choice of filling. Season to taste and set aside.

4 Deep-fry the potato shells (see Chef's techniques, page 63) until the flesh begins to brown, then drain on paper towels, skin-side up, for 5 minutes.

5 Turn the shells over, season the cavity with salt and pepper, then fill generously. If using the cheese and bacon filling, bake the jackets for 5–10 minutes, or until the cheese melts and the top is browned; alternatively, brown under the grill for 1–2 minutes. The other fillings can be served at once, or sprinkled with breadcrumbs and quickly toasted under the grill.

Chef's tips To roast garlic cloves, place them in a small ovenproof dish with some olive oil, then bake for 15–20 minutes in a moderately hot oven 200°C (400°F/Gas 6). To use, squeeze the flesh out of the papery skin.

Be adventurous with leftovers: tuna, meat, chicken, egg salad, vegetables and even stews make wonderful fillings for jacket potatoes.

Darphin potatoes

This dish—a flat cake made of grated potato—is named after the chef who created the recipe. It is often served with beef tenderloin.

Preparation time **15 minutes**
Total cooking time **20 minutes**
Serves 4

4 medium potatoes
oil or clarified butter (see page 60), for cooking

1 Peel the potatoes and place in cold water. Heat a 25 cm (10 inch) heavy-based frying pan over medium-low heat.
2 Grate the potatoes to a straw-like thickness, either by hand or using a food processor. (If you are working by hand, shred the potato lengthways.) Work as quickly as possible to prevent discolouring, but do not rinse the grated potato as the starch in the liquid will help keep the 'cake' together.
3 Add 2 tablespoons of oil or clarified butter to the pan. Season the grated potato with salt and pepper, then squeeze out any excess water. Place the potato in the pan and gently press down into an even layer with the back of a spoon or spatula. Reduce the heat to low and leave the potato to cook gently, giving the pan a good shake to make sure it doesn't stick. If the potato is sticking, add a little more oil around the edges and give the pan another good shake or two.
4 When the edges begin to colour, turn the potato cake over using two spatulas, and press down again to even out the edges. Give the pan a good shake, and if the potato cake sticks, add a little more oil around the edges and shake the pan again. Cook until nicely brown underneath. Remove from the pan and drain on paper towels before serving.

Parsley potatoes

Boiled potatoes can be dressed in a number of ways to complement any meal. Fresh herbs are especially versatile, while garlic is great for hearty flavour.

Preparation time **15 minutes**
Total cooking time **30 minutes**
Serves 4

4 medium waxy potatoes
60 g (2 oz) unsalted butter
I tablespoon finely chopped fresh parsley

1 Peel the potatoes and cut them into quarters, then turn the potatoes following the Chef's techniques on page 62.
2 Place the potatoes in a large pan of salted water, bring to the boil, then reduce the heat and simmer for 20 minutes, or until the potatoes are tender to the point of a knife. Drain.
3 Heat a pan over medium-low heat. Add the butter, then the potatoes, and toss gently. The potatoes will release a little moisture. When the moisture has almost evaporated, the butter will cling evenly to the potatoes. At this point, remove the potatoes from the heat and gently toss in the chopped parsley before serving.

Chef's tips If you don't have time to turn the potatoes, use small, evenly sized new potatoes instead.

The parsley can be replaced with any fresh, chopped green herb such as basil, chervil or chives. If you are using strong herbs such as mint, tarragon or coriander, decrease the amount to 1–1 1/2 teaspoons.

To make garlic potatoes, add 2 teaspoons chopped garlic to the butter in step 3. Fry the garlic for about 5 minutes, without browning, then toss through the drained potatoes.

Darphin potatoes (top) with Parsley potatoes and variations

Anna potatoes

Traditionally cooked in a round, two-handled baking dish, this recipe is named after a fashionable woman living during the reign of Napoleon III.

Preparation time **45 minutes**
Total cooking time **45 minutes**
Serves 4–6

1 kg (2 lb) potatoes
250 g (8 oz) clarified butter (see page 60)

1 Preheat the oven to hot 220°C (425°F/Gas 7). Peel and trim the potatoes, then thinly slice them using a sharp knife, or a mandolin set at 2 mm (1/8 inch) (see Chef's techniques, page 61). Place the slices in water until ready to cook.

2 Rinse the potato slices in cold water and pat dry with a paper towel. Heat 60 g (2 oz) of the butter in a large, non-stick frying pan over medium heat. Add some potato slices—not too many: they should be able to move around easily in the pan—and roll them in the butter for a few minutes until well coated and hot. Strain the potatoes, return the excess butter to the pan, and repeat in batches until all the potato slices are done. Set aside for about 5 minutes, or until cool enough to handle.

3 Coat the base of an ovenproof frying pan with 60 g (2 oz) of the butter. Leaving the pan over low heat, add some of the potato slices, arranging them in slightly overlapping circles. Season with salt and pepper, then arrange a second layer of potatoes on top, this time overlapping the slices in the opposite direction. Repeat until all the slices have been used, seasoning after each layer. Drizzle the remaining butter over the top, then transfer to the oven and bake for 30 minutes, or until tender to the point of a sharp knife.

4 To unmould, pour off any excess butter. Place a plate or platter over the frying pan and, in a single motion, turn it over. Serve immediately.

Potato and cream cheese fritters

These fritters are simple, versatile and delicious. Serve them with beef, or try them as an appetiser with apple sauce or fruit chutney, or for breakfast with bacon and eggs.

Preparation time 20 minutes + 15 minutes soaking
Total cooking time 15 minutes
Makes 12–14

250 g (8 oz) potatoes
60 g (2 oz) cream cheese
2 eggs, separated
pinch of dry mustard
oil, for cooking

1 Peel the potatoes, coarsely grate them and transfer to a bowl. Cover with cold water and soak for 15 minutes. Drain and pat dry on paper towels or a tea towel.
2 Mix the cream cheese and egg yolks together until smooth, then season with salt, freshly ground pepper and dry mustard.

3 Whisk the egg whites in a small, dry bowl until stiff peaks form. Carefully fold the egg whites into the egg yolk and cream cheese mixture, then fold the grated potato into the egg mixture.
4 Heat 2 tablespoons of oil in a large frying pan over high heat. Spoon 1 tablespoon of mixture per fritter into the pan. It should be possible to fry four fritters at a time, but ensure they are spaced well apart. Press each fritter with the back of the spoon to flatten it slightly. Fry for 3–4 minutes, or until crisp and golden brown, turning once during cooking. Drain on crumpled paper towels, then transfer to a wire rack in the oven to keep crisp and warm. Repeat with the remaining mixture. Serve warm as a side dish or as a starter.

Chef's tip Chopped chives or shredded leek may be added to the cream cheese mixture in step 2.

Tortilla

This thick potato omelette is offered in slices in tapas bars and cafés all over Spain, and each region has its own variations. The original, although seemingly plain, is delicious. This is a quick recipe that can be jazzed up according to your imagination.

Preparation time **15 minutes + 25 minutes standing**
Total cooking time **25 minutes**
Serves 4–6

125 ml (4 fl oz) olive oil
3–4 medium potatoes, peeled and cut into 1 cm
   (¹/₂ inch) cubes
1 large onion, thinly sliced
8 eggs

1 Heat the oil in a 20 cm (8 inch) ovenproof frying pan. Add the potato cubes and cook over medium heat, without colouring, for 7 minutes, or until tender.
2 Add the onion and cook for 7–8 minutes without colouring. Season to taste with salt and freshly ground pepper, then strain and reserve the oil. Place the potato and onion mixture in a bowl to cool for 10 minutes.
3 Beat the eggs, season to taste, pour over the potato and onion mixture and mix until well coated. Leave to stand for 15 minutes. Preheat the oven to moderately hot 200°C (400°F/Gas 6).
4 In the same pan, heat 1 tablespoon of the strained oil over medium heat. Pour in the potato and egg mixture, spreading the potato evenly in the pan. Cook for about 2 minutes, then transfer the pan to the oven and cook for 4–6 minutes, or until the egg sets around the edges, yet is still soft in the centre.
5 Take the pan from the oven and shake it to loosen the tortilla. To turn the tortilla over, carefully slide it onto a plate. Place the pan over the tortilla, then flip the pan and plate over: the cooked side of the tortilla should be nicely coloured. Cook over medium heat for 2 minutes, then bake in the oven for 2 minutes more. Remove from the oven and slide onto a clean, warm plate. Slice into wedges and serve hot, or at room temperature.

Chef's tip For a dash of extra flavour, sauté some bacon or sausage with the potatoes. Alternatively, add some sautéed vegetables or a little grated cheese.

Chef's techniques

◆

Perfect potatoes

For the best results when cooking potatoes, be aware that there are different kinds of potatoes,
and that some varieties lend themselves to certain types of dishes much better than others.

Some recipes specify the use of new, waxy, firm-fleshed, floury or old potatoes. Such distinctions can sound bewildering, but rest assured: they are not. The basic distinction to make is between waxy and floury potatoes.

Waxy potatoes are high in moisture, and contain less starch than floury potatoes. They have relatively thin skins and a yellowy, almost waxy flesh. Being firm fleshed, waxy potatoes boil well and will not come apart if cooked a few minutes longer than recommended; they also make wonderful salad potatoes and are perfect for casseroles and rösti. However, they are not much good for mashing or making into chips. Some varieties of waxy potato include bintji, Jersey and pink fir apple, as well as potatoes labelled as 'salad' and 'new' potatoes.

Floury potatoes have a low moisture and sugar content, and because they are high in starch, they fluff up nicely when baked or mashed. They turn golden when fried or roasted, and are good for making chips. Most 'old' potatoes are floury. Russet (Idaho), spunta and nicola potatoes are some common varieties of floury potatoes.

If all else fails, some good all-purpose potatoes will generally help you out: King Edward, desiree and sebago.

Whatever variety you buy, choose potatoes that feel firm and heavy to the touch, and discard any that have soft spots, sprouting or discoloration. Always reject potatoes with green skins, as they have developed an alkaloid that can result in illness.

Store potatoes in a cool, dry place away from light, and always remove them from any plastic packaging they may be sold in as the plastic will hasten their deterioration. Remember too that while the potato is a highly nutritious vegetable, overcooking and bad storage will destroy nutrients, especially vitamin C.

Clarifying butter

Removing the water and solids from butter makes it less likely to burn.
Ghee is a form of clarified butter.

To make 100 g (3¹/4 oz) clarified butter, cut 180 g (5³/4 oz) butter into small cubes. Place in a small pan set in a larger pot of water over low heat. Melt the butter without stirring. Skim the foam, without stirring the butter.

Remove from the heat and cool slightly. Pour off the clear yellow liquid, being very careful to leave the milky sediment behind in the pan. Discard the sediment and refrigerate the clarified butter in an airtight container.

Slicing by hand

Trimming and shaping potatoes before slicing helps give an attractive, even appearance to the dish.

Peel the potatoes using a vegetable peeler or sharp knife.

Using a potato peeler or sharp knife, trim the potato to an even shape.

Using a large, sharp knife, cut the potato into slices about 2 mm (¹/8 inch) thick.

Using a mandolin

This time-saving device has adjustable blades for slicing, shredding and waffle-cutting.

Attach the potato to the mandolin guard. This will make it easier and safer to work with.

For thin slices, work the potato against the straight blade, set to the thickness specified in the recipe.

For long thin strips, work the potato against the shredding blade.

Hasselback potatoes

Cutting large potatoes in this way ensures even, quick cooking, as well as impressive presentation.

Slice off the base of the potato to steady it. Make deep, thin parallel cuts across the potato, reaching almost to the bottom. The potato should hold together like the pages of a book.

Making gaufrettes

Gaufrette means waffle. These potato baskets are used to hold a variety of vegetables and garnishes.

Arrange the thinly sliced potatoes in the larger basket, and place the smaller basket inside. Holding the handles firmly, carefully lower the baskets under the hot oil and fry until golden brown.

Turning potatoes

This technique gives a lovely, uniform appearance to potatoes and ensures they cook at the same rate.

Cut the potatoes lengthways into quarters.

Holding a potato quarter in one hand, use a turning knife or small knife to trim off the edges and corners.

In a curving motion, cut the potato from top to bottom, turning as you go. The classic shape is oval, and about the size of a small egg.

Continue turning the potato portion until you have a uniform shape.

Puréeing potatoes

Potatoes may be puréed in several ways—but do not use a food processor as the result will be gluggy.

Hold a sieve securely over a bowl and press the cooked potatoes through using a wooden spoon.

Place the cooked potatoes in a mouli set over a bowl. Turn the handle to force the potato through.

Push the cooked potatoes a little at a time through a ricer, into a large bowl.

Making potato croquettes

Fluffy inside, and crisp outside, croquettes are a lovely way of using up leftover potatoes.

An easy way to divide the croquette mixture into even portions is to make a cake out of the mixture and cut it into even slices. You can then shape each portion to the required shape and size.

Gently toss or roll the croquettes in the flour, and shake off any excess.

Dip the croquettes in the beaten egg, then in the breadcrumbs or almond mixture, shaking off any excess. If the mixture is a little too soft to hold its shape, coat again in egg and breadcrumbs. Refrigerate until ready to cook.

Deep-frying

Fill the fryer only one-third full of oil: do not leave it unattended. Dry food thoroughly before deep-frying.

Preheat the oil in a deep-fat fryer or deep saucepan to 180°C (350°F). Place a bread cube in the oil: if it sizzles and turns golden brown in 15 seconds, the oil is hot enough.

Place the potatoes or croquettes in a basket and carefully immerse them in the oil.

Deep-fry in batches until golden and crisp, according to the time specified in the recipe. Shake off the excess oil, drain on crumpled paper towels and keep warm on a wire rack, uncovered, while frying the remaining batches.

Published in 1998 by Merehurst Limited, Ferry House, 51–57 Lacy Road, Putney, London SW15 1PR.

Merehurst Limited, Murdoch Books and Le Cordon Bleu thank the 32 masterchefs of all the Le Cordon Bleu Schools, whose knowledge and expertise have made this book possible, especially: Chef Cliche (MOF), Chef Terrien, Chef Boucheret, Chef Duchêne (MOF), Chef Guillut, Chef Steneck, Paris; Chef Males, Chef Walsh, Chef Hardy, London; Chef Chantefort, Chef Bertin, Chef Jambert, Chef Honda, Tokyo; Chef Salembien, Chef Boutin, Chef Harris, Sydney; Chef Lawes, Adelaide; Chef Guiet, Chef Denis, Ottawa. Of the many students who helped the Chefs test each recipe, a special mention to graduates David Welch and Allen Wertheim. A very special acknowledgment to Directors Susan Eckstein, Great Britain, and Kathy Shaw, Paris, who have been responsible for the coordination of the Le Cordon Bleu team throughout this series.

Managing Editor: Kay Halsey
Series Concept, Design and Art Direction: Juliet Cohen
Editors: Katri Hilden, Alison Moss
Food Director: Jody Vassallo
Food Editor: Lulu Grimes
Designer: Annette Fitzgerald
Photographers: Joe Filshie, Chris Jones
Food Stylists: Carolyn Fienberg, Mary Harris
Food Preparation: Michelle Earl, Jo Forrest, Kerrie Ray
Chef's Techniques Photographer: Reg Morrison
Home Economists: Michelle Lawton, Justine Poole, Alison Turner

Creative Director: Marylouise Brammer
International Sales Director: Mark Newman
CEO & Publisher: Anne Wilson

ISBN 1 85391 765 6

Printed by Toppan Printing (S) Pte Ltd
First Printed 1998
©Design and photography Murdoch Books® 1998
©Text Le Cordon Bleu 1998

A catalogue record for this book is available from the British Library.

Distributed in the UK by D Services, 6 Euston Street, Freemen's Common, Leicester LE2 7SS Tel 0116-254-7671 Fax 0116-254-4670.
Distributed in Canada by Whitecap (Vancouver) Ltd, 351 Lynn Avenue, North Vancouver, BC V7J 2C4 Tel 604-980-9852 Fax 604-980-8197 or Whitecap (Ontario) Ltd, 47 Coldwater Road, North York, ON M3B 1Y8 Tel 416-444-3442 Fax 416-444-6630
Published and distributed in Australia by Murdoch Books®, 45 Jones Street, Ultimo NSW 2007

The Publisher and Le Cordon Bleu wish to thank Carole Sweetnam for her help with this series.
Front cover: Darphin potatoes (top) with Potato fans with bacon and Parmesan

---

IMPORTANT INFORMATION

CONVERSION GUIDE

1 cup = 250 ml (8 fl oz)
1 Australian tablespoon = 20 ml (4 teaspoons)
1 UK tablespoon = 15 ml (3 teaspoons)

NOTE: We have used 20 ml tablespoons. If you are using a 15 ml tablespoon, for most recipes the difference will be negligible. For recipes using baking powder, gelatine, bicarbonate of soda and flour, add an extra teaspoon for each tablespoon specified.

CUP CONVERSIONS—DRY INGREDIENTS

1 cup flour, plain or self-raising = 125 g (4 oz)
1 cup sugar, caster = 250 g (8 oz)
1 cup breadcrumbs, dry = 125 g (4 oz)

IMPORTANT: Those who might be at risk from the effects of salmonella food poisoning (the elderly, pregnant women, young children and those suffering from immune deficiency diseases) should consult their GP with any concerns about eating raw eggs.